DON'T GIVE UP,
GIVE IN

Author Name: Carol Barbara Boccaccio
Publisher Name: Carol Barbara Boccaccio
Contact Information: cbboccaccio@gmail.com
Website: www.CarolBarbaraBoccaccio.com

Don't Give Up, Give In/ Carol Barbara Boccaccio. —1st ed.
ISBN 978-1-7388195-0-8

DON'T GIVE UP, GIVE IN

A PETIT MEMOIR BY

Carol Barbara Boccaccio

DISCLAIMER

This is a work of creative non-fiction. The stories in this book are true. The events, and locales are described in such a way as to maintain anonymity and protect the privacy of the other persons therein. Therefore, the author has omitted names and changed identifying details and characteristics throughout the book. The conversations in this book all come from the author's recollection, however, they are not written to represent word-for-word transcripts. Rather, they are retold in a way that gives readers a sense of the essence of the dialogue, and in all cases, this is accurate.

This is also a petit memoir – meaning that it is not a full-length memoir. There are many other events and experiences within the timeframe of this story and beyond that have shaped the author and the views and perspectives she shares and doesn't share in this book. The author personally preserves utmost compassion, respect, and love for all of us on this Earth. We are all moving through life's challenges and beauty, together.

Furthermore, the content of this book is for reading pleasure, only. The opinions, ideas, and experiences expressed within these pages are not meant to be followed as a guide to any one person's healing journey. The author recognizes that each person is unique and whole in and of themselves; Each person's choices and the reasons for their choices are theirs and theirs alone. Neither the publisher nor the author shall be held liable or responsible, whatsoever, for the ways any and all readers digest this information and/or apply it in their own lives.

To all readers, please seek advice and support from your trusted healthcare providers for your personal mental, physical, and emotional health concerns and struggles.

Some of the author's mentors and spiritual guides have been referenced in the book for those readers that are curious to explore more. Enjoy.

CONTENTS

This one's for you, Libs.

Don't Give Up, Give In

Don't give up, give in.

What's happening in my life is a door.

Walk through.

Find ease.

Simplify.

Be with my animal body.

Breathe in.

Breathe out.

Breathe in.

Take another look.

Don't Give Up, Give In

"Between a rock and a hard place"

In the beginning, it felt like pushing a massive boulder that had been sitting in one spot for probably millions of years. But it needed to be done. With whatever energy I had, I began to build momentum.

I grew up privileged. I lived most of my childhood in a safe, suburban, predominantly white neighbourhood as part of a white, middle-class family in Canada. I was given and I had a lot, and I learned to work hard in the ways my parents did with little to worry about. I also grew up gifted; I had advanced potential in many areas in my life from very young. I was an ambitious student and athlete, and I excelled at everything I put myself into. I was social and vibrant and prided myself on being able to connect with most people around me. I had a plan to continue being "successful" in my life.

But when I got to teen-age, the ground underneath me wasn't as sturdy as I was expecting, given who I was and all that I had. The vibrancy and motivation I felt as a girl started to diminish when I began pursuing my budding sexuality as a young woman. And I wasn't feeling the way I expected to feel when I was being met in that way. This began impacting the way I walked and asserted myself in the world. Furthermore, I didn't feel the support I was expecting in order to pursue who I wanted to be in the world. The pressure to chart a post-secondary school path that would give me the biggest financial security possible was clouding what my true joys were, at the time. Together, these two things left me feeling very unsure about myself, and about life.

Then, when I left that phase and entered adulthood – chartered path in hand – a violent event in my life completely de-railed me. I dropped out of a prestigious university degree and I lost my connection to everyone in my life. From one day to the next, I was like a sweater whose one loose string got pulled into a total unravelling. Everything from my sleep, concentration, and diet, to my social and active life became thwarted. I tried to hang onto what was left with total denial of what was actually happening. Survival mechanisms in my brain and biology took over, so that I couldn't actually process the event, or its devastating after-math on my life and mental health for some time. Over a few years that followed, I continued to live numbly through several other traumas –assaults and abusive circumstances – until my collapse was so heavy, it was impossible to ignore any longer.

This story starts here. There are times in life when we are "between a rock and a hard place" as they say. We suddenly find ourselves stuck somewhere or with something that we had never intended to. We fight it and we question it and ourselves because it just feels so untrue to us. And yet, here we are. And we can continue living there with lies, and excuses or bargains with ourselves. Or we can actually listen and look at our lives with a new set of eyes in order to change. Akin to being an animal in the wild whose senses are suddenly heightened because they need their next meal, we too, start to tap into a wilder resource within us that can sense which way and how to go and what to do.

This is what happened to me. This is where I fell into what I needed to heal, understand myself and my world better, and keep going. I didn't give up, but I gave in.

I gave into where I was in my life and how I was feeling. I gave into the despair, I gave into the massive loss and victimhood I was feeling. I gave in to hope like a boat with no oars. And in doing so, I found a way forward. Slowly, yes, but surely. It was like learning to ride a bicycle. It takes some practice, and then suddenly we have the wherewithal to keep pedaling, and there was the key all along to stay up and stay balanced.

What I found was a message: Follow your bliss. Follow your heart. And I listened. I listened closely to what that meant for me at that moment in time. I gave in, and I let it guide me.

Our true be-ing is always micro-moments ahead of us, leaning through the doors of a wilder and wiser self.

15

* * *

I'm harvesting parts of my story into a tiny book because I want to put it down in order to start a new one. I want to validate myself, the last 15 years, and some of the ways I have grown through the sticky mud of it all, and found beauty again. My overarching intention for myself is to put my story down in a way that really harvests the wisdom out of hard times.

I'm here with you because I have a voice that wants to help others on their own path and with their own stories. As an author, my intention for the readers is to provide a new lens for overcoming struggle, and encouragement for finding our own journeys around coping.

Here in this petit memoir I lay some of my pain, and I share what I gained from it. My hope is that you find and feel Validation, Confidence, Connection, Patience, Gratitude, Kindness, Compassion, and Empathy for your own journey – whatever that is.

I want you to know this story. That I've been created to see these events in a way that ultimately frees me and us all.

I want you to know that you can trust your self and you can trust the world that you are an essential part of. I want you to know how I came to this, myself. That I've walked this path. And there is a way through without suppressing our inner emotional selves. And without having to force anything either. There is a way to having it all.

Keep going. Start a new story. Then start a new one. And a new one. As a cherished counsellor once expressed this idea so well to me: "There doesn't seem to be an end point most of the time. Our life stories go more like this: Once upon a time… And then, once upon a time… And once upon a time…"

I want you to follow your heart. I want you to get lost in the beauty. I want you to be kind.

And remember: We all come from a place to get to another place. Wherever you are in your life… it's okay.

Come sit at the table.
Come as you are, right now. Come
with all your triumphs and foibles.
Come together, come alone. Come
empty, come full. We are each one a
part of the all.
Come feast.

Planting trees

---

*And your green never looked more
green than after the rain.
Have you ever seen the desert green
after a hurricane?*[1]

At the end of high school, I would have these strange
sentiments in my room when I was alone that I
wouldn't live past 20 or 22. I had this feeling like I was
going to die. I even recorded a random video of myself
on my computer saying that. And I was right. But it
wasn't a physical death I experienced. It was the death
of life as I had known it then.

I was turning 22 and I was alone with very few friends
still in my life, but I had finally left an abusive partner
for good. The last meet we had was in Quebec where I
had gone to spend my birthday with an old co-worker. I
conceded to meet with him and decided I'd try to gently
confront and express to him about how his behaviour
affected me and encourage him to find some help. He
walked out on the lunch bill, left me to pay it, and then

he stalked me for 6 blocks before I lost him in a metro station. That was the last time I saw or spoke to him; the man I considered my first adult love.

I was suffering the effects of complex post-traumatic stress he, and other men in those prior years had left with me. And I wasn't actually aware that that's what it was at the time.

I was severely depressed, isolated, and in a state of complete physical and nervous system collapse. I would download shows and movies, and spend entire days in my bedroom numbing myself with black-screen entertainment. I'd sleep 12 hours a night because I struggled facing the day, facing my life, and all the time I was losing. I didn't want to live in the world. I could barely walk out into it.

I felt like a huge failure for being as depressed as I was and unable to lift myself out of it. Every move I made felt monumental, and it was. In the scheme of some of the events in my life and lack of support I had or allowed myself to have, that I survived that time in my life is incredible.

If I got up to do anything, it was to binge eat some food, or take a walk to a park, or the library, or art supplies store – remnants of dreams to become an artist still anchored somewhere inside me.

I was also still suffering the occasional panic attacks and tunnel vision that had started when I was first attempting to leave that abusive and controlling relationship. And these attacks built an incredible amount of fear in my body and in my mind. At times, I didn't know who or where I was in the middle of the panic. The agony of those attacks felt like I was going through a psychosis every time, with the primary thought being, "I'm dying."

And I wanted to die. But I wasn't ready for it. I'd have these thoughts of running in front of a moving truck or bus just before it passed me. I'd constantly be telling myself "I don't want to live anymore." But I couldn't even do that – commit suicide.

I gave into those sentiments, though, yes. I gave myself totally to them, because I didn't have much strength most of the time to do otherwise. I remember lying in bed, feeling so exhausted, and thinking that if I fell asleep, that I might die from the despair I was in. And so every time, I'd have to reconcile my own will to die somehow in order to fall asleep.

And on one particularly hard day near my 22nd birthday, that I still remember vividly in my mind, my heart was pounding in my chest with every slight move I made. I couldn't get myself out of my head and I couldn't get myself out of my bedroom door. It felt like my whole body was being cemented into place. I couldn't bear turning another calendar year like this, feeling so alone. I was ready to die. And I totally broke down under the weight of that truth.

I didn't give up. But I gave in.

I grabbed the only line out that I could feel around me. For me, that was to call a clairvoyant. I had been talking to one woman in particular a number of times in the previous year. I had found her after initially seeking out a "spiritual guide" online. And when it came down to it, a seer seemed like the only person that could hold all the confusion, uncertainty, and despair I was in, and give me hope. She could give me over-arching ways of looking at my situation and my life and give meaning to it. This would gently guide me and my energy toward ways to heal, grow, and ultimately change. And I did believe (and still believe) in an empathic interconnectedness that made reading other people's lives possible. And somehow, feeling connected to her and believing in what she offered me, gave me hope. It was a hope that the logical/material world – and its people – tried to give, but had failed. I needed someone that could pull me out of my detached state while keeping me tethered to possibility.

I called her. This woman on the other side of the line, after listening to several minutes of me just crying, just crying, and maybe also squeezing in an "I can't do this anymore," she said to me:

"Follow your bliss."

I felt like I had seen that before. I had recently been visiting Joseph Campbell's body of work. He talks about how following your bliss is really just listening to who we really are. And how our lives can transform simply by choosing to follow the path that our felt-sense bliss guides us toward. And in that open-ness to feel and pursue goodness, and be led by it, we might be surprised by what opportunities and events open to us.

"Follow your heart," she told me. She said it several times in a row as if to really drive it home to me. And then she said, "I see you going out to the west coast for a job."

The only bliss I could find in those days was when I managed to get outside, leaned my back against a tree, and took a moment to breathe. I'd inhale deeply and visualized as if I, too, was the sturdy trunk of a tree, and I felt my core as something strong, and rooted. This was a meditation a hypnotherapist had offered me back in Quebec. And it was the only thing a therapist offered me at that time that stuck with me. A tree meditation.

In Quebec, I'd walk home from appointments or work and stop at the small pockets of parks scattered in the city. Taking the moment to lean or sit against a tree, I was comforted by its gritty exterior texture and the solidity of its trunk against me. I appreciated the thought of air being so gently and lovingly exchanged between my lungs and the tree's like the perfect union of life that we are. And I really took to the company of the tiny songbirds that dwelled them. The birdsong seemed to put me in the same hypnotic state as that therapist. I'd look inward and feel my core as something just as sturdy as that tree. I'd focus on my breath until the noise of the city was drowned out. Those moments of feeling something strong and safe but alive relaxed me enough to rest into a few moments of stillness in my mind.

From those foundational silent conversations, trees became the only presence in my immediate world that could offer me the slightest peace.

Nothing and no one else could. I was living in my mother's basement in Toronto, but no one in my family could reach me, even if they tried. And all my friends had left my life and were busy with their own. Therapists at the time had tried, but there was nothing there for me or for them to work with. I couldn't understand why I was the way I was.

So, I followed that connection to nature I started in Quebec, and I began spending more time with trees, again. I spent more time outside at the parks, at the lake, sitting up against trees, letting myself breathe and soak in their towering, judgment-free presence.

Within a week of consciously connecting with trees and the grace it offered me, someone mentioned a cool job they had heard about to me: tree planting. I went online, researched for two days about it, and was hooked. I sent out dozens of applications there and then. It was the first company I applied to that called me 24 hours later, interviewed me, and gave me a job.

I took it. I scrambled to make enough cash to get me out there. Three weeks later I landed in Vancouver, BC. And I never looked back.

Of course, there were people that tried to convince me not to do it, that I wasn't ready, that it was going to be too hard – and all manner of scenarios that tested my state of heart. But after having just lived in the gates of abuse and control and beginning to set my mind and body free again, a fire fueled me to put opinions – even well-meaning ones – out of my influence at that time. I needed myself more than anybody else.

I couldn't doubt the sudden burst of motivation I had to leave Toronto and spend a summer in BC forests. A sense of liberty and ambition beckoned me! It was the first time I had felt that sort of drive since playing sports in high school. I missed it. An energy inside me was back. I didn't know for how long. And nothing was really in the way of it. Most of my life had been cleared out of almost everything and everyone at that point. And looking back, I'm now really grateful for that. It allowed me to start again. And so I did.

Here was that moment. The moment when I was on the cusp of rebirth. And that moment is one of complete and utter chaos. And there's nowhere else to go but straight into it. The life behind me is already gone.

It was just like being a baby in mama's belly, there was a moment when there just wasn't enough room to grow anymore.

I didn't necessarily know where or how to go, but I knew I had to. So I gave into the moment. And suddenly, somehow, there was an opening. I was so clear an opening and a pull, that there wasn't a need to doubt it. Birth is as final as death.

So whether it's an exit, or an entrance, or both, I walked through.

A pilgrimage

[She] slipped briskly into an intimacy from which [she] never recovered. – F. Scott Fitzgerald[2]

A few of the other ladies in camp and I would joke that he was the camp candy. How can a single woman not swoon over an exotic accent roaming through camp.

But if I'm honest, I wasn't actually that interested so much as I was interested in how much more fully I was living my life, then, that summer, for the first time since pre-adolescence.

I felt like myself again. Easily socializing, engaged in the music that I loved, fully excelling physically at this new job (one that has been compared to Olympic training!), making money, totally capable, feeling free and independent surrounded by miles of wilderness. I was buzzing with a sense of goodness that I hadn't been open to for so long, especially by this point in the work season. I had gotten over that first big hump of learning to plant a tree fast and well, and I was just flying.

There was also something really special about being at the 60th parallel, where we were planting. The land of the midnight sun in the peak of summer. It was mid-July then, so the night fell for only about 5 hours. The days were long and hot, and there seemed to be a stillness in the air from it all.

Wildfires that broke out filled the sky with smoke, and you could literally stare at the sun. In the mornings it was the most beautiful and eerie orange globe hanging over the skyline.

And us planters would be wading knee deep in swamps with our bags filled with hundreds of trees, evading the bugs. But whenever I'd take a moment to look up and look around, there was something about those lands that teemed with presence and beauty. Maybe it was the towering cottonwoods that they left standing in the cut-blocks. The wild roses and aster flowers dotting the miles of flatland. Maybe it was the moments between adrenaline-soaked hours of pounding trees into the ground that were saturated with stillness and beauty. I don't know. But every time I get a whiff of swamp smell, or feel an arid heat on my skin, I'm transported back to that time and all that I was feeling.

It made meeting him all that much more potent, I think, ultimately. I began just making conversation with him in line for a meal one day because I could see he kept mostly to himself. We would have our morning and evening meals just getting to know each other and shooting shit about our days, engrossed with others at the table in conversations. It was so easy and pleasant. Everyone at that camp felt like family at the start and end of a long day.

After healing from a repetitive strain injury in my back, he lent me a spare mattress from his trailer. So when he suddenly had disappeared from camp on a call to another contract, I left a note with his colleague thanking him for the mattress and asking to stay in touch in case I was ever in his neck of the woods. I expected nothing.

And yet, we spent both of our last nights in that remote town together. Again, having expected nothing but maybe a drink, the night took off. One drink to the next. And finally, back in his room, he leaned in to kiss me. A kiss that felt like it lasted forever before an item of clothing even came off. That night remains the most incredible night spent with a man in my life, and I couldn't even tell you why at the time. It just was. No one had ever treated me, my body, my pleasure with so much presence before – and I was open to it. On my face pasted a smile that couldn't retreat from the softness of his touch, and the passion of his presence on and inside me.

I knew it was just one night, but I didn't anticipate THAT night.

I was high – literally high – for about five weeks afterward. And when I finally came down, it hit me like a ton of bricks that I was overflowing with love from/for this man.

We had said our goodbyes already, he had informed me of a life he needed to go back home to and figure out. We both knew we had our separate paths to travel. Still, I had to tell him how I was feeling and what was happening to me as a result of that night with him. I didn't even know the fraction of it yet, but I told him what I could, because the magnitude of that love and gratitude I was feeling was impossible to ignore or bottle up.

It's a beautiful thing when you love somebody.[3]

The combination of having started a new life, and then having experienced that calibre of a man sent me flying onward through the opening that had unfurled in the months prior. I was following the momentum and where it was leading me.

It became clearer that I was letting myself go. Not in the sense of "letting go of something" like I am letting go of a ball in my hand to watch it drop to the ground. Letting "go" like letting a bird that had been shellshocked from an encounter with a window shake it off, get up, and fly away – *go* – again. I was letting myself go with love that was growing in my heart. For myself, and for this man.

This man and my love for him became a sacred gateway in the year that followed. It was essentially my own love and capacity for love that I was getting to know, and turning it inward again. Looking back now, it makes sense that we couldn't be together, because for me, I had the more important task of turning the beauty and bigness of my love around toward myself. It was truly a gift to meet him.

Over the course of the rest of the summer, myself and a good friend I had made from the planting season took off to find more work, which really just ended up in more fun, and a worry-free freedom to roam through summer's long days and enjoy what came our way. I made rich friendships and memories that summer. And when I was asked what I'd do next, I knew I would travel.

Someone suggested I continued on tree planting through a contact of hers in Australia. And I said yes!

Within a week's time, I had decided to fly to Brisbane. I applied for a work-stay visa, got accepted, and booked a flight for a week after that. Without much money left in my pocket from the summer, I went to Australia without a plan, but a faith imbued with a love that was impossible to ignore. A love that inspired me to find my way through everything, come what may.

My trip to Australia was spontaneous. And everything that occurred on my travels was spontaneous too. I was surrendered to something greater, free of any ties. If I had a plan to go north, something would happen or I'd meet someone that would encourage me to go south. And ultimately, one experience after another, I met the people that would take me on a journey deeper into myself, my life, my body, in order to discover who I really am, what matters, and how to radically accept and love myself.

This man I had met I wouldn't see again. And all that love that I was letting myself feel for him got funnelled into my own individuation journey. It fueled me to keep going, keep believing, and keep walking through the openings that presented themselves.

Letting go of a plan freed me to experience the world through a different modus operandi. One that lent itself to grace, the kindness of strangers, the trust of my own capacities of discernment, and the magic weave that holds all of us interconnected on this planet. The kind of oneness that has a power all its own. I got to see and know that power and that entity intimately reflected inside of myself. The courage that sent me flying through, and ultimately as that opening, is Love.

Courage comes from the French root word: COEUR, which means heart.

I didn't force the love I felt away. I could have. After all, he was elsewhere and tending to what he needed to. It would have been easy to throw the baby out with the bathwater. I drained the water, but I kept the baby. I hadn't felt that good in almost a decade.

Fall in love. Stay there. – Rumi[4]

I didn't care if he wasn't there. I was feeling something wonderful. And I let myself ride it. I am still riding it. I took it all the way. It's got a different shape now. The shape is me and all that comes my way. But I feel Love as the most true thing that exists.

And when that got tested, I held to my truth, and Truth itself was more greatly illuminated. Love IS the way. Love IS the bliss. At least for me, that's what it is.

Over the course of that pilgrimage in Australia, I surrendered to what my bliss wanted to show me. I led myself where I needed to be led and trusted what appeared. What I learned on each leg of that journey was ultimately what I needed to keep choosing the path that was closest to my heart and my being in the world.

On that journey, I met a gift of a man I now consider had been a lighthouse in my life. He housed me when I landed before having even met me, and via his book collection, I was led to my most important spiritual teacher. Osho's book *No Water, No Moon* pointed to what such a deep surrender I was embarking on would ultimately lead to.

I met an organic farmer from Malaysia that further illuminated the path of enlightenment for me.

I spent time with an artist and a clay field therapist that gave me my own hands back – ones that could make sense of the past and fashion a path forward for myself.

I sat for a few weeks with a healer and her pack of dogs and puppy litters. Her presence was a blessing – she was in the midst of her own healing and re-birth.

I connected with an autistic boy that taught me more than all the people I've met in my life combined – radical acceptance, connection, believing. This seven-year-old boy and his gifted little sister showed me the doors in my own mind to experiencing enlightenment.

I stayed with a shaman who led me deeper still, who tested my faith, and who showed me that I have a voice, and that my voice is beautiful. The forests of her property extended for acres, and were temples for my dancing and singing.

And I met the most giving heart who reminded me of how to honour nature, my woman's body, and the simple wisdom of caring.

Because he wasn't there to absorb my love, my lover was everything and everyone that presented itself to me, and I poured myself into each moment. I surrendered to loving everything and everyone as best as I could, including myself.

As with all things love, friction arose. And the friction only turned my tires over the pavement and led me onward into what needed to come next.

The deeper I surrendered to this spiritual journey, the deeper I found and felt myself. I developed a steady stream of actively meditating on my love and the ever-changing environment. From this, my consciousness grew and grew, until I awoke to include it ALL as "me." Experiencing Love in this way melted the borders of my identity into a crescendo moment (almost exactly one year after my big breakdown) that changed my perception of life forever. What I experienced was enlightenment. And the journey I had always been surrendered to became coming back to that *sacred* moment in present time through loving the self that showed me the truth of who I am.

If that's not true love, I don't know what else is.

Sexual healing

---

*The human body is a phenomenal
creation. And there's a tender heart
drumming at the centre of it all.*

As with all journeys up a mountain, the road must come
down again. And falling in love and experiencing
enlightenment didn't actually change the path I needed
to continue travelling in order to keep healing, and to
ground myself and my new self-knowledge.

After my trip to Australia, I came back to live with my
mother in Toronto for the winter, and I landed with a
big thud; heavy with new experiences I'd gained and
still carrying a big ole backpack of old ones. Being back
in the big city after over a year spent deep in the bush of
BC and Australia felt jarring and cold. I was much more
sensitive to sound and the presence (or lack there of) of
space and wilderness. I could hear the clanging and
screeching of the streetcar from home at all hours of the
day, the rainfall felt grimy and metallic on my skin, the

breaths that I was taking were shallow and not nearly as refreshing.

Winter was approaching, and I was back to moving through deep valleys of depression and immobility. I clung onto threads of experience I had discovered during my time away and the re-connection I was opening to my bliss and my pleasure. And like the lifeline that this intimacy was, I began enrolling myself in Tantra workshops and courses.

I needed to understand better how it was that one man's touch could change my whole relationship with myself and the world around me.

"Alright folks, I know it's just a craisin, but stay open to the possibilities here."

We were each given a single dehydrated sweetened cranberry and holding it in the palm of our hand with puzzled, innocent looks on our faces. *What's this got to do with my sexuality?*

"Begin by simply gazing at it. We'll spend a whole two minutes here, and with each of these successive steps. What catches your eye about it? Notice how you relate to the craisin."

I give in to the exercise. I start to observe the intimate details of this shrivelled little fruit between my index finger and thumb. I become obsessed with the garnet hues, and the tiny seeds that remain plump in contrast to its flesh. I notice sweet oils sweating onto my fingertips, making it more mobile between my touch.

"Now put the craisin to your lips without putting it inside your mouth. Let your lips explore the craisin."

I suddenly see what this exercise is all about. I'm having a long, slow love affair with a craisin. I immerse myself into the encounter. Curiously, I feel a deep yearning to have and be with this craisin like it was a long lost lover, as I continue to explore it pressed against my lips, anticipating its taste. Two minutes go by in what feels like seconds.

"Go on and put it on your tongue, now, but no chewing! Just leave it there."

My breathing deepens as I lengthen my desire to keep it slow. I allow myself to salivate for two minutes, sucking up the juices, and feeling more embodied in my tongue than I have ever been in my life. My tongue becomes this entity all its own. And I start to see the implications of this exercise not just on sex, but on my relationship to food, to sound, to challenges, to all life. I see how much I can be conscious of and feel. The nuances of pleasure and bliss that can be discovered when slowed way down are infinite.

I find myself curiously sweating from the heat that's growing in my body. *Is this craisin giving me an orgasm?*

"Okay, you can chew now, but make it last two full minutes. No swallowing!... yet."

The class is giggling. Some are having a hilariously awkward experience or have already eaten their craisin. Others have gone deep into their sensual curiosity and are glowing. All of us are learning and revealing something very intimate about ourselves in one way or another.

By the time I am asked to allow myself the experience of swallowing the craisin, there are only the seeds and some juices left. I'm vibrating as I sit there, eyes closed, feeling it slide down into my belly. My whole body seems so alive, awake, and sharp. The sound of my throat, my breath, and the sensations are intense and bright. I'm pulsating.

I just finished having sex with a craisin. And a quiet stillness overtakes me for the last couple minutes of the exercise. I'm profoundly struck by the experience.

A second course series I attend soon after that is a women's group that focuses on growing our capacity for and intensifying our orgasms.[5] In a home exercise I find myself doing after the first class, I am asked to touch and give loving attention over 20 minutes to every single part of my body.

When I begin, I find myself easily rushing through it, thinking about other things, bored and disconnected.

Hmm... disconnected. I can start to see how far away from my own body I keep myself.

I remember the craisin exercise and so I slow it right down. I start again with my big left toe, and I focus on its subtle form and beauty. As I touch my toe, I am surprised to feel my toe touching me back. And as I move from one curve and body part to the next, a silent bond begins to form between my heart and the rest of my body.

By the time I am touching the contours of my eyes and nose and head, silent rivers of tears had carved a forgotten story on my face, and pooled itself on my breast above my heart. And I'm slightly shaking from the vitality, and the awareness I'm gaining in relationship to a loving touch and to my body.

* * *

I love how Jungian psychologist, Clarissa Pinkola Estés[6] speaks of how the body remembers things. How it might only be the slight graze of a finger on skin that opens the gate to a memory held there-in.

`The body remembers everything.`

Something broke free in my mind. And during these first couple months of enrolling myself into Tantra study and exploring sexuality more sacredly, I began being able to review memories of sexual violence in my past.

I suddenly grew an immense need to discuss one particular memory with my psychologist. And I realized that underneath my choice to find a male psychologist that year was this desire to confront and discuss my relationship to men, and what had actually happened to me in the years prior.

By this time, it had been five years. And I finally felt safe and secure enough to re-member and talk about a sexual assault I was surviving from when I was 18. My mind kept it totally buried for five years. And the doorway to this was ultimately beginning to deeply honour my sexuality as a woman.

I can remember the session with my psychologist like it was yesterday. I am holding a pillow to my belly, as I usually did when I arrived to help me feel grounded and soften into the space. There's a gentle dappled light coming in through the tree branches behind the window pane, offering a golden glow in the room about us. I feel safe here. I tell him, "You know... I've got this memory coming up of an experience I had with a man that I think I want to talk about because there's a lot of shame attached to it."

And I go on describing a really tough memory whereby I had had unconscious sex with a stranger during my first week of university in Quebec, and the next day, I was so badly bruised internally, and externally around my neck and hips, to the point that I could barely move without groaning in pain. I couldn't walk, sit, or go to the bathroom for days. I couldn't stay up. "And all I can really remember from that week was sleeping for enormous amounts of time, and then getting very sick and going to the hospital with pneumonia."

My psychologist just looked back at me speechless.

I immediately needed to fill the silence. In his pause, I took the opportunity to speak more to how ashamed and guilty I felt, blanketing the horror I was feeling with something more manageable in the moment. I said that I "must have allowed it to happen because I didn't stop it." I was gripped by this massive shame and sadness I was feeling around it all. In the cloud of confusion and emotional pain I was in, I couldn't understand why.

He asked me if I understood what rape or sexual assault was. And I thought I had, but in my pain and the state I was in, I wasn't reconciling what had happened without taking responsibility for it.

My psychologist had to educate me on consent. What had happened to me was an aggravated sexual assault. And also beyond what I could have controlled at the time. It's not that I didn't stop it, it's that I couldn't. Over several sessions, I struggled understanding why I had a hard time letting go of shame and saying so.

> *It's the scrutinization that women
> get far surpasses the scrutinization
> that men get.* – Lisa Ling
> (featured in Miss Representation)[7]

So, he guided me toward this documentary to watch called *Miss Representation.* The film opens with the quote:

> *The most common way people give
> up their power is by thinking they
> don't have any.*
> – Alice Walker[8]

Miss Representation exposes the effects of sexism in the media we consume and the world that young girls grow as women into. When I took this in, along with many more videos, talks, articles, and books on 'rape culture' and other feminist issues, my perception of myself and the world I lived in completely shattered. It began to fill a gap for me about the powerlessness and voicelessness I felt in relationship to men at the time, and also, how it was that a man could be so violent with me.

> *These images are part of a cultural
> climate in which women are seen as
> things, as objects. And turning a
> human being into a thing is almost
> always the first step toward
> justifying violence against that*

The documentary, especially, opened my eyes. I remember watching the endless rolls of film and images that revealed how poorly we represent women in the media we consume; our objectification, commodification, and sexualization in all manner of mediums from music videos to magazines and advertising; the questions and comments made to female leaders about their beauty, age, bodies and femininity; movies and video games in how they depict and normalize violence against women. The number of harrowing statistics – alone – that this documentary revealed, left me shaken into a much bigger awareness.

I remember thinking "How the *hell* did I miss this? And why are we letting this happen?" But really, how *could* I see it. I was still in a state of hell from traumatic stress and our culture's overarching impacts on me and my life. And no, it's not that we are letting it happen, it's that in growing up to meet it is when we are least discerning and most susceptible to its harm – girls and boys, alike. And then, the healing journey is what it is from there: an unknown wilderness we are having to map ourselves through to get home to the true power of ourselves as human before gender.

The documentary also features a letter written by the American Psychological Association to the US. Department of Health and Human Services. The report that is detailed in the letter says:

> *Sexualization and objectification undermine a person's confidence in and comfort with her own body, leading to emotional and self-image problems, such as shame and anxiety... Research links sexualization with three of the most common mental health problems diagnosed in girls and women--eating disorders, low self-esteem, and depression or depressed mood.*[10]

I saw myself in every woman in that film. I'd always been objectified and valued primarily for what my young, female body can do for men and capitalism. To some, I'd always been a sexual target. And I was raised to believe that a woman's pleasure and experience in sex was much less important than, if not nil in the presence of a man's.

> *That [men's] needs get met first in relationships with women; that's not genetically pre-destined. That's learned behaviour.*
> – Jackson Katz, PhD (featured in Miss Representation)[11]

Between hearing the opinions, experiences, and voices of other women, young and old, of discriminating and supportive, good men, and reviewing the constant stream of media I am immersed in with a new lens on how women's potentials are consistently being thwarted and abused in our society (consciously and unconsciously), my personal experiences became momentarily clearer, but not easier. Simultaneously, I finally felt found, and also deeply alone in a sea of madness.

* * *

I go on diving into all sorts of practices and courses around bringing more consciousness to my sexuality. At every turn, I find myself battling resistance and sudden freeze reactions that completely take me away from my intentions.

I find myself riding these waves of wanting more of this divine love I had gotten to know and following that desire into all sorts of work around my sexuality and healing past relationship dynamics. And so I'd also be falling into deep valleys of depression and dissociation when I'd have to face memories of my past. And I needed that down-regulation in order to rest and digest from the realities I was penetrating – in order to keep surviving. This dissolution process felt like I was battling a fever. My head was clanging between hot and cold. I was a spirit floating between the past and what I wanted to create for my future.

The work I was engaged in was overcoming years – if not centuries of ancestral influences – of an illusion of powerlessness that was fed to me as an ideal. And I did so by going heart-first into it and accepting it.

It would have been so easy to give up at this phase. Awakening to repressed memories, patterns of sexual violence and misogyny, not just in my own life but in the world at large was/is complex, heavy and overwhelming. All I could do was yield to it while I inched my way into greater empowerment and vitality, again... through orgasms. And through seeing my sensuality as something more than simply sexual, but something that connects me to life around me, and the goodness of what that life has to offer.

When I lie on green grass at the start of summer, it's my skin that picks up on its freshness, its coolness, and it's softness. It's my nose that engages with the flowers on spring's evening air, sending me swooning. In winter's sharp clarity, my eyes reveal to me an endless night sky of sparkling miracles of life, and it's my ears that partner with the silence to bring me home to the peacefulness of that image. And it's my heart that chooses *these* memories to keep.

In other words, I could see then that my senses and 'sensuality' are really just the edge of who I am, meeting the world. And that this skin was being re-grown through my sexual healing.

I continued to resolve bringing more pleasure, safety, and bliss to this area of my life. And I found a ton of support through the traditions of Tantra, Taoism, and other spiritual disciplines that hold sexual energy as sacred and as a pivotal part of human evolution and cultivating consciousness.

And so, as I was reclaiming my sexual energy and using it to better myself and my life, I could see that it mattered... A LOT.

Slowly, I grew this ability to believe that I matter, my pleasure matters, my voice matters, my body matters, my choices matter, and my experience matters – and how little control I've had and still had over that. Purely from the world I inherited at birth.

This phase of my life was about finally having built enough strength, balance, and grace to face what happened, how I was derailed, and allowing that old skin to start to fall away. And learning that the way for that to happen is by feeding the newness of being.

Liberty

I was on the Toronto streetcar coming home from work along Queen St. We pass the "LIBERTY SHWARMA" take-out restaurant. And I tell myself that if I get a dog one day, I'll name her Liberty.

Some weeks later, I'm at a dear friend's who also lived in Toronto at the time. We'd become friends while tree planting my first season. I was expressing to her how hard it was that winter to get out of bed in the morning and get going. She knew I was battling depression.

"Get a dog!" she said, as we were both cuddling with her own newly adopted pup. "Get a dog. You need to get up to walk the dog every day. It will help you get moving."

I immediately received that as a pretty darn good idea. I knew I would someday get my own canine companion. And I had even decided on a name for that dog.

This friend of mine had recently suffered a huge loss in her life in the previous year. "I wouldn't be able to get through my days without my dog right now. And I'm so grateful for it. A dog will give you a focus that you otherwise don't have in your life right now. It will change your ideas about things."

I followed her advice onto Kijiji that evening and in the days that followed. I looked for a border collie cross-breed. And then I saw her: Liberty. A beautiful black and brown-cheeked border collie and blue heeler pup. When I called the ad, the woman on the other line had the same name as me. I took it as a sign. I knew then that I would go out to meet her.

The pups were already eight weeks old when I found the ad. And so one week later, I went to go meet her in Kitchener, and I left with little Liberty in my arms, a little scared of the decision I had just spontaneously made.

But there was no turning back, not then, and not since.

There have been SO many bumps and roller coasters on this road, on this healing journey, on this path I chose for myself. At times it was hell, at times it was heaven. And there were many, many times when I felt regret over missed opportunities.

When I look at my girl, Libby (short for Liberty), I remember what it's all for. It's for Love.

I fell so deeply and strongly bonded with Libby from the start. As a pup, she was so incredibly wild and full of energy, she easily took up 75% of my time. We'd go on massive walks, and I devoted myself to training her to be ready for the next planting season a few months later. It was a lot of work. We spent all day, every day together and we grew very attached to one another. We still are.

This decision I made to have Libby in my life has directed my path in ways I never would have expected. Sometimes painfully; finding pet-friendly housing in BC has been such a struggle, and I've found myself living out of my car multiple times so that I can hang onto her – to us. But interestingly, choosing our bond led us to living in the most beautiful corners of this province and finding life-long inspiring friendships along the way. And while I had to make tough decisions, and experience certain set-backs and losses, ultimately every turn my life took because of having her, freed me further and led me to a more sublime and true horizon. This taught me a lot about standing strong in who I am and what I want, choosing what I care about – what brings me joy – and the field of unforeseen magic/circumstances that can occur about me when I do so. Again, here was this concept of following my heart and bliss into the unknown and discovering immense strength.

The love I grow for Libby is stronger every single day because I choose it every single day. And I learn just how powerful Love REALLY IS! Every decision I make for her, for us, is infused with a beauty that is so impossible to ignore, that no matter what happens, I truly make the most of it, and turn it into an experience that nourishes me deeply and frees me. And *wow* – does it ever!

It started by just getting up in the mornings (or in the middle of the night – as new mommas know so well), and getting outside in the dead of winter for long walks together. And onward, every day her presence has encouraged me to get up and get moving – polishing my edges against the grit of the day!

Libby has witnessed me in my darkest nights, and she has always been a cushion to land on, giving me a softness that I can always depend on. I still wake to her, daily, snuggling her head into my neck or on my chest responding to my *"good morning, baby girl"* with her own resonant toning.

She also knows how to keep me on my toes and engaged. As a herding dog ancestrally, she always wants to be engaged in an activity and be praised for it. She learned her major commands like "come" and "stay" within our first two weeks together. And from the first time I threw a ball for her, she was hooked on fetching it back to me for another. She's incredibly intelligent, and she doesn't let me ignore that intelligence. I can see myself in her in that way. When I work toward my potential, I'm including hers and what she deserves, too. We are One, and she is a reflection to me in so many ways. I feel like she speaks to what is still possible and gratifying if I keep meeting life's challenges as she does; with an enthusiasm for more!

There isn't a day when Libby doesn't make me smile or feel gratitude. And this alone, has added to the bank of bliss that has kept me moving forward toward more.

Spending time with animals and in nature teaches me something so fundamental about who I am. In its pure simplicity, Nature nurtures a wonder that need not be explained, just lived. Beyond anything that my mind has the potential to be, my nature, my body, has the capacity to be SO much right here, right now. I am imbued, just like Libby, with senses that are connected to this moment alone.

We are nature. – Steven Hoskinson
(Organic Intelligence®)[12]

And this moment, when I enter it fully, is SO rich, is so nurturing, and is so saturated with Love. Love in the form of challenges. Love in the form of simple birdsong or breezes. Love in the form of views that soothe me. Love in the form of beautiful daydreams. Love in the form of my breath, and its steady beat, in and out. Love in the form of needs. Love in the form of touch. Love in the form of words. When I am willing to surrender, to receive it, Love goes on and on forever, showing me that all that aliveness need not be beyond this very moment.

Libby is a sacred portal for that kind of wisdom. She is a bridge for the love I still have to give and the love I am here to receive. In the hours that I needed to choose life, I chose her. And in every challenge I've had at maintaining a decent life for her and for us, I chose giving into the love and gratitude I have for her. She reminds me to choose virtue every time no matter how hard it is because it's *my* nature. She makes me that much more important. She reminds me what I am living for: goodness, health, beauty.

She reminds me who I choose to be: love.

Love is so free. Thank you, Liberty.

Love is the only miracle there is.
Love is the ladder from hell to
heaven. Love learned well, you have
learned all. Love missed, you missed
your whole life. – Osho[13]

Living the wisdom

---

*Peace is simply about shedding
what's between us and being Here.
Let the heavy cloak fall to the
ground. Let the way be clear.*

Surviving trauma is one thing. And I think many of us can live our entire lives simply surviving some of the events and sometimes drawn-out experiences we are subject to – whether that is abuse, neglect, oppression, loss. Understanding, digesting, and releasing our personal trauma is a next thing. And then, feeling safe enough to come out of hiding and more fully into being alive is another thing entirely.

I learned that trauma is an unconscious process that I needed to become conscious of, not just to be free of it, but to make use of it in a way that increased my life instead of reducing it. And although I've mentioned "trauma" several times in this book already, at this particular point in my story is when I was only just starting to use that term for my own experience.

I was doing the work. Cycles and waves of debilitating mental health continued to ensue in my life in the winters that followed. Certain depressive episodes still threatened to take me out, but I had something I was living for that kept me tethered to surviving with more conviction – Liberty. And I had found a job that could hold me, heal me, and energize me in the summers – tree planting.

Finding my way back into the world in a way that felt authentic, embodied, and self-loving was like feeling my way through the dark. I knew how I wanted to feel. Without knowing exactly where to go, this was the path I could travel.

So, I'd still find myself easing into old comforts and habits. In the winter, that was binge-watching TV and emotional eating. And when I did have some energy in Spring and Summer, I'd find myself dating whatever men were available to me purely for the relief from being alone. And to keep moving in the right direction, it was absolutely necessary for me to cycle through this in order *to* choose what was right and true for me.

* * *

Choice is an example of something essential that I had lost in the years of becoming a woman amid abusive circumstances and events. I became physically scared of making the wrong choices and therefore setting myself in motion, too. And this has been a major cause of frustration and impatience with myself. But it was important. Every choice I made because I consciously felt and knew I wanted to was important, mattered, and made me and my actions stronger.

I'd be at the grocery store for two or three times as long as most other people because it could take me fifteen minutes just to choose what rice I wanted.

"Do I want basmati rice? Do I want jasmine? Jasmine is fluffier when I make it. But then basmati might be nicer with these veggies I bought. Maybe I need to choose different vegetables... Do I want white or brown rice?... Hmm... What do I want to make with this? Do I really need rice?... I guess I should get organic. But it's expensive!"

Then I'd get anxious from standing there with three different kinds of rice in my hands while five other shoppers already came and left with their choices. I'd start having an anxiety attack, have to put all the choices down and walk away, and come back after getting another item.

I felt ridiculous. This happened a lot with all sorts of situations where I had to make decisions. Some really banal. But these were all moments when I had to be patient with myself and consciously call on my will to choose "me" for my mental and physical health.

* * *

Part of who I created myself to be throughout childhood was this exceptionally engaged human being. And I wanted to feel that again. I wanted my potential to fill me and express itself through me. I didn't want to let those qualities of me go. It was a special kind of bliss that I clung to. And I didn't want to believe that it was gone or part of the past that I had lost.

I was still carrying the child that thrived off of excelling, but also pleasing the status quo. This *idea* of excelling and success still had a grip on me and I hated that I wasn't moving faster towards maintaining the responsibilities that I was *supposed* to have. At least this is how I conceptualized my losses at the time – I couldn't yet understand that the bliss I sought going back to was actually just the bliss of being more fully in my body and in the moment with confidence and ease.

Simultaneously, I was also learning how much more truly at odds I am with a status quo that didn't honour feminine nature. Healing in the midst of a world in need of healing is an alchemical process, not a destination.

Still, because my mind couldn't let go of where I thought I should be, it would funnel into my moment-to-moment experience as intense self-judgment, self-repression, and denial. I couldn't go out, be with friends or family, and have fun because I really believed the state I was in was ugly. I felt like a sickly wolf moulting its fur coat. And I was! But in my mind, it meant I wasn't worthy of being amongst the more beautiful and vital people of the world.

I physically couldn't be in their world because of my nervous system responses, and the anxiety I was in – I was fearing my own embodiment. But my mental thought process behind it just kicked me further down into it.

"I can't let people see me like this... I don't even want to see myself like this... I did this to myself. I'm so stupid... I'm boring... I am uncomfortable to be around... I'm not ready, yet... I'm going to drop out again if I try and go back to school. I'm only going to disappoint my family, again, if I do... Don't go out! Don't move! No! Don't choose that! That's a bad idea!... I am a failure."

I wasn't good enough. What I was doing was not good enough in my mind.

It's SO hard to see this process of reconstituting oneself as sacred and beautiful when the world emphasizes and spotlights what is grand and youthful and shiny.

Instead of choosing the things that brought me joy, I wouldn't think I was good enough for them. Or if I didn't have certain good things in my life, I made it mean that I must not be worthy of them, yet. I'd be focused on what's wrong. And listen, no one can survive with this kind of broken record.

I remember surrendering deeply to this one day. I needed to spotlight my own mind to see what was going on. I took my journal, and I drew this little circle in the middle, and then in the next circle around it, I wrote

"I'm so ashamed." And then in another circle "Failure" and "Loneliness." And the next, "I'm not okay." And on and on, I let my negative thinking run its course until the page was a tornado of self-deprecation.

I looked down at it and cried. I closed the journal, I curled up in bed, and I cried. Libby jumped up and cuddled me, and we just held each other in the long, sad moment of my own defeat. I fell asleep from the heaviness I had placed onto myself.

When I woke up, I opened the journal again. I took another look – a compassionate look – and began erasing the words in each circle, and re-writing them: "My pain is beautiful." And: "It's okay." "I love my smile." "I revere me." And then "Love" in all the last circles that surrounded the inner ones. Just love. Love. Love. Love. Love.

I noticed as I looked down at the newly-refurbished page that it was as if I was looking at the concentric circles of the stump of a tree. And I immediately felt held in that image. And I cried new tears. Tears that released me.

I began realizing how important these tasks were. I needed to immerse myself in my own love, trust, and positive regard – not just when I'm flying in the sun off of good feeling, but especially when I'm walking the shadowed valleys of my pain and disappointment.

* * *

Compulsive self-disregard and emotional repression are never deliberate or conscious.
– Gabor Maté, PhD[14]

Becoming aware and turning these thoughts that attached themselves to my psychosomatic state took a lot of energy and time. Remember that million-year old boulder? My mind and body would regularly tap me out. And the relief I'd get, most of the time came from more TV and food. When I'd hit a block, I'd usually find myself either going on a baking rampage and binge eating what I made, or I'd be firmly fixed to my computer screen binge watching a show I downloaded. Or both.

As mentioned, I wasn't always aware of engaging these behaviours. Most of the time, when I was in such a deep state of depression, a system of survival was taking place in the more animal part of my brain, reducing my front-brain thought processes to a bare minimum amount of engagement. I couldn't problem-solve.

And yet occasionally, through the different tantra and active meditation practices I was engaged in, moments of clarity to my own behaviour would open up, giving me an opportunity to change.

I slowly and begrudgingly began to lean into my compulsions too, as they presented themselves. Whatever greater intelligence pushed me to do that, I allowed it to open those binge episodes as a new experience for me...

The job is enjoyment. And it really is
a job, sometimes.
– Steven Hoskinson (End of
Trauma™ Course, OI®)[15]

I'm in the middle of eating my 5th brownie in less than an hour after baking a batch and I'm smacked in the face with what I am doing. First, because I felt the shame in what I was doing, next, by just noticing the shame and bringing compassion to my detached state.

Instead of hating myself for picking it up and eating it, and instead of refusing myself, I pause, and I slow it right down. I feel it on my lips. I feel it between my teeth as I'm chewing and as my mouth salivates and moves the flavours over my tongue. I feel what I'm eating go down my throat and into my belly.

The whole thing turns into an immensely sensual experience filled and bursting with life. I start to imagine a hole inside me being fed with love. I tell myself how bodacious and beautiful I was eating so much chocolate like that and I dramatize my indulgence a little further. And this makes me laugh. I enjoy the huge smile suddenly pasted on my face, and I can feel my whole body relax. The hairs on my neck lift. I let out a sigh.

I'm full! So full, in fact, it hurts, and a connection to my body takes over. I settle into that experience, letting my lower belly hang way loose. I place my hands over it as if I've got a precious little babe in there. I imagine myself as that precious little babe. And I giggle again at my own imagination. I feel my eyes widen as I silently honour just how lucky I am to be in a position of filling myself up to such an extent – and so humorously. Gratitude fills what was formerly an experience of self-disgust, for the first time in my life.

In that moment, binge eating became SO much more than just a symptom of deteriorating mental health – denial, repression, or distraction. It was an opportunity to be more aware of my body and mind, and to accept myself. To learn to receive and give to myself freely, and connect with the immediate physical and sensual world with beauty and goodness. There's bliss here, too.

> *Under the right conditions our*
> *biology becomes auto-organizing*
> *(that means self-organizing).*
> – Steven Hoskinson[16]

Over time, my eating habits naturally improved and changed to be in greater service to what was more deeply true: I'm not hungry for food. I'm hungry for "me." And I'd channel those urges into something creative like dancing or writing or taking Libby on a beautiful hike. I channeled emotionality into my guitar and came out with these incredibly beautiful songs that spoke to my life experience.

Whatever I did that I didn't like but couldn't help, I began to imbue those experiences with consciousness and meaning. I slowed them down in my mind so that I was in the physical experience – an opportunity to hold myself and my truth. And in whatever beauty was presenting itself and being reflected before me. And with each new beat, I grew. I was healing.

I now knew a bit more about where my immobility was rooted into: a massive and complex disconnection from my body, and essentially from pleasure. And I also knew a path I *could* keep taking: through. Cycle after cycle of experience presented itself to me in order to be healed of these roots. And I'd catch a wave whenever, if ever, I could.

Each wave I caught was an opportunity to live the wisdom I had and was still gaining from going fully into the moment – however painful or beautiful – with love.

* * *

Eventually, I found myself in a new relationship. It was the first since my previous abusive boyfriend. Going into this relationship was big for me. It was an important step in my self-love. And while the relationship was utterly destroyed, I was absolutely successful.

I had chosen to pursue a man who made me smile and feel really carefree. I loved him but I found a couple of his closest friends highly misogynistic and really didn't like the way they spoke about women and engaged in porn. He also loved porn and had been watching it for a long time.

I began to have what I would come to know as acute post-traumatic stress episodes. I was having night terrors and waking up shaking next to him. I became hysterical sometimes and unable to regulate my emotions – especially anger and anxiety. I would lose my memory constantly and forget what I was doing or wanted to do – which scared me and made me feel like I was going insane.

The ways he and his friends would speak of women, of me, and the porn and men's culture they were engrossed in was triggering me into these episodes immensely. In the middle of sex, I noticed he'd disconnect or do something really oddly misplaced, and I'd have to stop immediately. I became kind of repulsed by him sexually despite asking for my needs to be met and trying. The sex we were having, the memories it was all bringing up was making me dissociate very strongly.

Flashbacks were enmeshing themselves with my present reality. Because I couldn't show this man I was with the acceptance he needed, I rationalized that I was becoming my previous abuser, which made me panic and review the past constantly in my mind. I was in a storm of confusion, hypersensitivity, and reactivity that I had no control over. And for reasons I could only understand later, I was unable to leave. This forced me to find the words to my experiences and my story.

I began going to a support group for women who had been in abusive relationships, and also going to a new female counsellor who specialized in trauma. This was really the beginning of coming to define and understand "PTSD" and my mental and physiological health issues as symptoms arising from the impacts of trauma and toxic masculinity on my life. It was also the beginning of learning to say no.

Speaking more honestly about my experiences to a female counsellor, and as a woman to other women, hearing their experiences, was re-mapping the bigger picture of my life and what was happening at the time. This treasured counsellor led me to an extensive and fantastic resource called *The PTSD Workbook*, which I could only take tiny bites out of, but that deeply nourished my understanding of myself and my behaviour.

Shortly after ending this relationship, I had a massive opening in my voice. I went on to open up completely about my past with a dear friend of mine in the most honest and vulnerable way for the first time outside of therapy. This was when I began to feel safe enough to claim my version of my story and my strength to speak my truth.

Here's an excerpt from a journal I kept at the time:

> *"I realize that I've been avoiding really just looking at my trauma. I'm identifying the problem through the ill acts of [this man] and his friends, as opposed to my own experiential lens. [He]'s gone, now. He made me realize just how prevalent traumatic memory is in my life. Now I need to gain greater understanding of me, my patterns, my relationships, my choices. And how all this [discord] and all this work is ultimately leading me to the life I deeply want and have within me to create."*

Of the relationships that followed, each one succeeded the next. And I knew I was finding healing. Because I could say: "I need this" and "I deserve this," and choose it over a relationship that refused to grow in ways that would truly acknowledge my needs and desires. Holding my ground interpersonally ultimately led me to making the seemingly inconsequential decisions of everyday life (like what rice I wanted) much easier. I was saying yes to being in my body and its asks of me.

Intimacy, especially, became a space in my life to claim a deeper wisdom I was gaining about self-acceptance, and what bliss meant to me and my body. Pieces of me and the life I was re-creating for myself came through these relationships. Over and over again, they offered me opportunities to choose differently and develop personal power. They helped me to continue developing the important skill of speaking up about my truth. And to come home to myself.

* * *

The cold comforts I was defaulting to as I journeyed on were ultimately the cornerstones that pivoted me toward the ways I needed to give to myself.

Before I could choose that which truly gave me bliss, I had to enter the territory I had been accustomed to, again and again, to see the roads, take and make new ones, and create a better roadmap of who I wanted to be and how I wanted to experience it.

And whenever I hit a wall, again, I'd have to see it as another opportunity to: be conscious/observant, surrender, connect with myself, and find what's true – as best I could in the moment.

If I wasn't giving up yet, then I was giving in.

It was always enough, there was always something to be gained by staying the course. If only a grain of sand's worth. If only millimetres of the road to where I truly desired to be, who I deeply knew myself to be. If only awareness, or a few seconds of peace, or of a true love I was manifesting from inside me. If only to survive the day in hopes of a better one.

This period of my life took a long time. I was cycling through old habits/comforts/relationships in order to *truly* live.

And in the process of re-patterning those cycles, I created a way of travelling that would become the journey itself. Loving what is.

We are right to be hopeful

Life is a series of natural and
spontaneous changes.
Don't resist them; that only creates
sorrow. Let reality be reality.
Let things flow naturally forward in
whatever way they like.
– Vernon Howard (on Taoism)[18]

Before I knew it, twelve years had passed since my life
as I had known it had been swept out from under me.

I was turning 30 in the new year, and this landmark was
providing a clear lens to look back at my life through.
For twelve years I'd been oscillating between
beautifully grounding in the now and in ease, and
fighting with what was happening to re-create myself
back into someone I could feel proud of.

So much time passed. And I felt like I lost so much time.
I remember looking at people I had grown up with and
where they were in their lives – starting families, in
successful careers, purchasing homes – and I felt such

MASSIVE grief for the life unlived; the life that I had been expecting. The one my mind thought I wanted.

When I saw three weeks go by, and all I could do on each one of those days is get up, shower, and do the bare minimum of feeding myself, my dogs, and taking them on a walk, I'd feel very sad for myself.

When I looked at all the relationships and friendships that had failed due to my mental health issues or simply because I could not make authentic choices and voice my truths, I felt lonely and grieved the ease of that sort of company.

When I looked at my body and the way it was changing, I grieved not having been able to share it with another body, not being able to use it for all the athletic challenges I've always yearned for, and not having been able to make more use of the strength, power, and energy of my youth.

I grieved not having been able to be in the world because it had already been a decade of learning to be with myself and I was still learning. I felt like I was still dragging myself through a bog.

I dreamed of another life ahead of me, and the more time passed, the more I realized I needed to adjust my ideals to make room for the reality of my dis-abilities.

The grief at this landmark in my life was HEAV-y.

When some areas of my experience improved, others worsened.

My menstrual cycles had grown incredibly painful and debilitating. I was suspected to have developed endometriosis. And from my perspective, likely due to all the trauma I was carrying in my pelvis. I also developed other chronic pain issues that were just starting to worsen. There were days when I couldn't move or get out of bed without crying from the – now, physical – pain I was in.

On the other hand, my mental health had improved significantly, by this point. I was able to ride the waves of winter with more ease. I had found beauty in simplicity, again, and in the little day-to-day consistencies in my life. I really could look out onto the world and say "Life is beautiful." Tea in the morning outside, listening to the birds whistle a tune. Moving with the weather. Walking along the lake and watching the sun glisten over the water. The pregnant silence of the forest. As one of my favorite novelists, put it, that which is most wonderful in life is usually that which is most simple. A lot comes from connecting with nature, and letting that moment be enough.

And also, simple daily routines I had gotten into that fed me. I was writing a lot, doing yoga, eating well, keeping my space clean and tidy. I was playing guitar and singing as an emotional outlet. I was building personal music playlists again – something I had loved doing growing up – and dancing regularly. I also stopped consuming junk media, movies, and TV. I'd fill my mind with ideas that came from mentors and authors I resonated with and deeply respected, instead.

I became much more conscious of the men and relationships I was choosing, if I was choosing any at all. And I was starting to speak up for myself in many places and claim the space that was me in the world.

I wasn't where others were career-wise, but I was here.

I meant to do my work to-day –
But a brown bird sang in the apple tree,
And a butterfly flitted across the field,
And all the leaves were calling.
– Richard le Gallienne[19]

Over all those years I found and developed ways of managing myself that led itself to more peace and wellness. I had slowed down. I was learning to see how the sheer amount of space I provided myself was helping me grow into an even better version of myself than I could have imagined.

With all this improvement mentally, I was now moving into a phase of physical disability. And to be honest, I wasn't surprised. I could feel it coming. I had spent so many years healing severe mental illness, that I was ready for the impact that holding tension in my body could manifest.

I was scared when it did begin. I thought maybe it was something much more serious, like cancer. And I kept the pain to myself for a while – I was too scared to do anything about it and find out what it was. I also deeply knew it was attached to healing my past, and this is never an easy thing to talk about to allopathic medicine practitioners.

One particular menstrual period I was having was remarkably difficult. It came with massive pain all throughout my chest and body. And I really thought that I was dying and that I would die alone. I had such a massive migraine that I was puking every day, and it was clear to me that I was releasing so much more than just that month's blood.

And all I could do was give in. I let myself lean into the comfort that the thought of death could provide me in those moments. And in so doing, I found myself discussing the life I had lived until then with myself:

I survived a horrific event, years of abuse, and kept going.

I lost all my friends, and tore myself away from all my close family relationships, but I found a deep foundational relationship with myself.

I surrendered deeply and I found Love.

I embraced depression as a door to what I deeply wanted from life, and away from what was weighing me down.

I became a deeply, beautifully orgasmic woman, not just sexually, but in a way tantric with everything my senses came into connection with.

I discovered the power of Spirit.

I put faith in virtue and trusted myself.

I re-membered my dreams.

I reconstituted my ability to intellectually understand and learn things remarkably well into a larger capacity to see the world, the universe, and my life in it with eyes of compassion and greatness.

I've discovered true moments of bliss – enough to make it all worth it; to give it all meaning.

My soul is good, I've made a good life for myself. I trust whatever is next.

I decided that if I was going to die, that I would at least comfort myself through it. I held my body for days and days. I just told myself: "It's okay," and: "The life I've lived is enough." "I'm beautiful," and "No matter what happens, I will love myself through it."

This happens. Illness, loss, gravity, confusion, suffering... being utterly lost in the world happens. Life and disasters can literally wipe our life – or life as we know it – away. And who's to say, now that I know, that that's not where life's true bounty exists?

When I emerged from that bleed, I felt so much clearer and more purposeful than I had ever felt in the previous decade. I felt an enormous amount of peace. I felt light. I felt an acceptance and perceived a beauty and depth and richness in that acceptance of life that I was able to carry everywhere with me, into every interaction with the world.

And I suddenly understood that there's nothing better than being in that steady beat of beauty I was giving myself and the world by just allowing what is, to be. I let go of what I "thought" life should have been and should go. I grounded in the now – and essentially, in ease – and I found everything I was looking for. I freed up a massive amount of space.

Now, curiously, I also found a new choice. It was no longer about surviving at this point. I was moving into the realm of living again. Simple, good living. Of choosing and learning to *really* love my self and my life, moment to moment and finding that I am rich. That there is so much on the horizon, and I need only take it one step at a time, if at all.

When we witness a flower in full bloom, we don't always see its process. It's a seed, and it needs what it needs: good soil, water, sunshine. But most of all, it has a timing all its own. It's not going to jump from green leaf to a thousand petals open. It's going to bud for a while, it's going to unfurl each petal individually. And you know what, it's probably because it's busy basking in it all – every struggle, every opening, every stretch, every inhale, and every exhale. The flower lives in the present moment.

The seasons – winter – IS a thing. And it's beautiful too. You don't see the trees pushing out leaves when the conditions aren't right. Let the energy go and develop elsewhere. Winter always swings into Spring.

Time heals. We are right to be hopeful.

Using my voice

*There is no greater agony than
bearing an untold story inside you.* –
Zora Neale Hurston[20]

I'm looking up an old flame on social media. And I notice
a gorgeous and happy little boy that looks like him in
his profile picture. My hearts seizes me as I consider
whether I will ever be able to raise a child.

At this point I am still unable to work throughout a full
calendar year, I'm living at the poverty line, and other
housing struggles added a ton of stress to my already
complex PTSD. I was unsure if I'd ever meet a partner
that could hold me, my past, and the work ahead – and
whose own work I, myself, could hold. I could lean into
the moment and the disabilities I was experiencing. I
could see and bathe in beauty and possibility. But I was
looking for a way to overcome the inertia I was in.

On this day, I opened a new door inside of me. It was
clear I was still keeping myself in the clutches of the

major assault I experienced in 2008 because I didn't want to accept that my life had changed forever and that I was still being affected by it. But it had, and I was.

I was a victim. And I needed to be able to say it and then let it go.

Throughout that winter I was doing a lot of work on being able to write and tell my version of the story of that night; learning to sit peacefully and beautifully with it. But all I kept constantly imagining was talking to my perpetrator, telling him how much that event royally screwed with my life and my relationship to myself. I was hanging onto an anger that I just didn't want to let go of. I wanted justice, and I didn't know how I was ever going to get it.

Because I had been so preoccupied over the years with all these horrid events and how to tell the truth about what happened, I wasn't allowing myself the space of actually letting it go. I wasn't ready yet. I was still reclaiming my voice. In the process of trying to tell my victim story, I was still *in* it.

It's a month or so before I'm turning 30. And I decide it's time to begin to consciously forget what happened and make room to choose a new story. And without a moment of trepidation, like an ember in my core becoming a flame, it occurs to me that the only way for me to do that is by reporting what happened.

I needed to create the strength to stand with my story, and also beyond it. I knew I wasn't going to be able to walk on without shining a light on this man, making a witness statement about what actually happened, and standing in the solidarity of other victims in the world. So that's what I did.

At a local advocacy centre to discuss if and how it is possible for me to report an assault over 10 years after the event, I was met with such a huge outpouring of love, support, understanding, and sisterhood by the victim support worker. Meeting with this woman really turned a new leaf for me. I was able to be totally and completely vulnerable with her. In that raw and exposed self I was presenting, she made me feel like I was the most powerful woman in the world. By her presence, alone. She understood because she, herself, had been there and helped dozens of other women through, too. She knew everything I was feeling and more. She knew what it meant for me to be there and taking steps back into my sovereignty in the world. And this was like opening the window to let the fresh air in, of a new story beckoning.

In our conversation, I mentioned to her how there are a few things I need to work through to be able to do this. A huge wall of fear about reporting him was blocking me from moving forward. She referred me to a community woman's counsellor to support me throughout the reporting process.

From day one, this women's counsellor was more direct with me than anyone else had ever been, especially in a therapeutic setting. I was totally intimidated by her audacity to be so present and honest. But this confidently probed me to put up a thicker skin and build up strength in my mind, whether she knew that's what she was doing or not. And it was exactly what I was going to need to get through to making that report.

In our first session, after telling her a bit of what happened to me, I remember really wanting to discuss this fear I had in reporting. A guilt about what it could do to *his life* peaked in my brain. I hardly got the word "guilt" out of my mouth before my counsellor interrupted me, looked me dead in the eyes, and said,

"NO."

I was baffled. Who did this counsellor think she was?

"No," she said. "*You* feel guilty? You?... You shouldn't feel guilty. He did this, not you. He's dangerous."

That word: *dangerous.* I didn't give it much attention, then. I was more shocked that she was even putting words to my experience, as a counsellor.

And yet, there was something in that interaction with her that rocked me so good to the core. No one had EVER been so bold and strong in showing me just *how wrong* my perpetrator was in assaulting me. And equally, how wrong it is, to have your voice robbed and ideas introjected to such a degree that saying "no", even a decade or more later, is still an internal dilemma.

I needed that. She shone a very important spotlight on me and my own mind.

* * *

And the day came
when the risk
it took
to remain tight
in a bud
was more painful
than the risk
it took
to blossom.
        – Anais Nin[21]

"There is actually one more thing I need to say."

I have no idea where this impulse comes from, I just know there's something else I need to say. Like picking up a piece of the puzzle from the box, and knowing exactly where it needs to go before your mind even processes a thought about it. It almost feels like magic, but it isn't. It's the power of being fully present.

I was talking to the victim services worker who is in close liaison with the corporal I made my initial report over the phone with. We were debriefing about how it went. It was about two weeks prior to that moment when the corporal had asked me the question over the phone: "Is he dangerous?"

I was already taken aback by the fact that she asked for his name during that phone call to report the assault. I wasn't ready for that. And now she was asking me *Is he dangerous?*! I didn't know how to answer. I fumbled between "I don't know," and "He could be," but "I don't know where he is or who he is or who he is with now." I really just couldn't answer it for myself or from myself.

And now I was coming into a sudden clarity as to *why*.

My heart rises with a courage akin to the sun dispelling a heavy cloak of morning fog in my mind. Clarity. And it's instinctual.

"I'm scared to say that he's dangerous," I said. "Because if I say he's dangerous, then to me, that means that I can't trust anyone in this world. That man was a complete stranger that battered my body, and stole the life I knew from me – and he pushed me back into the city streets like it was nothing to him."

I started to cry. I was coming up against a truth I haven't wanted to say, even to myself, for all these years. I couldn't stand living in that box anymore. I didn't even know I was, until that moment. It took using my voice to get there.

For twelve years I had been internalizing that I am not safe with anyone, and that what happened, and

who I am, are unimportant. The way my body and my mind shut down and hid to keep me safe all this time made a lot of sense in that moment.

* * *

A new strength pushed through, like a fresh petal claiming her space in the flower. It's her turn to unfold.

A month later, I went on to make a full two-hour report going over every single detail of that night I could remember with the corporal in person. I'm free of it. It's not in my hands anymore.

In the week that follows, my physical body goes through a massive transformation. I experience what seems to be a big bout of gastroenteritis. For days I'm vomiting constantly and expelling anything and everything I put into my body. I lose a ton of weight and get mildly dehydrated, to which point a friend takes me to the hospital to make sure there's nothing more serious going on.

I'm okay. And the episode passes. But again, it's as if my body had its own energetic release to process and express as a result of the statement I made.

Since then, since reporting my assault, I've been experiencing a massive resurgence of my vitality and motivation in the world. I haven't been held down by severe depression or fatigue in the same way since before using my voice in that way.

There was something so fundamentally essential for me, my presence, and the space I occupy in the world in the decision to report this man.

I finally got the chance to say "**no.**"

And: "I matter. I deserve to be heard."

It gave me my voice back. It skilled me in greater self-compassion.

Meeting my fears made me stronger and more self-trusting in the face of the cruelty in this world.

Advocating for myself freed me to express and pursue my true self, my interests, my desires, and my pleasures above anybody else's.

And choosing myself made me more empathetic and able to forgive.

In giving into my victimhood, I gave into my ability to say "no" to *it*, too. And see that I am also SO much more beyond the occurrence of trauma and always have been.

A new story

Dance The Medicine.
– Bernice Raabis[22]

I'm dancing another wave at a conscious dance class.

A radically free dance space is the place where it all comes together and makes sense for me.

Here, as in life, I don't know what music is coming, but I am committed to dancing.

I am taken on a journey and I am opened and deepened by it all.

Here, I am in my body, I am in my power, and I trust every way that I respond because I can see that every move I make is intelligent, beautiful, and weaves the tapestry of my life.

My body speaks before my mind gets the chance and I praise her for it. I celebrate by listening and letting her choose how she needs to move.

Here, the music and everything it represents is rich as fodder for my fire. The music is a story that reflects me, and I reflect the music. I am exposed to every emotion I am willing to call my own and dance with, learn with.

Here there's an interconnection I can feel with all things. There's one heart keeping the beat. There's a reason for it all, and it must be blissful because I'm still dancing.

Here, I can see my potential filled to the brim and overflowing.

Here, I can let everything go and just be in love with my body in this moment.

I dance to acknowledge. I dance to forget. I dance for the inertia it maintains in my life. I dance to find ways through the dark nights of my life. I dance to dream myself into new being.

I dance and then, I continue dancing off the dance floor. Because the dance is all there seems to be when I'm surrendered fully.

I dance because it feels good.

I dance because I'm alive.

I dance because deeper than anything, I am in love with being alive.

And I found that by giving in.

* * *

> *When a great ship is in harbour and moored, it is safe, there can be no doubt. But that is not what great ships are built for.* – John A. Shedd[23]

I'm walking the dogs with tension tightly knotted into every joint in my body. I re-orient myself to my surroundings and I notice the twilight colouring the clouds. A storm just passed. I am brought into a deeper inhale. A sigh relaxes my shoulders and I can feel my feet on the ground. They feel heavy in a very supportive and grounding way. And each step I take feels gently powerful.

I am learning to manage my pain. Mindfulness is a great friend. And I choose to be brave.

The challenge I face, today, is providing a safe environment for my dogs and helping them to heal, now, too. They've internalized my lack of safety and taken on a lot of my stress over the years. This asks me to look at how my relationship to myself is still being encouraged to grow in order to better support them and keep encouraging my own existence.

I love where I am and all that I've created in my life. I've learned to speak up; ask for support where and when I need it. I'm proud of who I am.

And... on this day, I'm noticing I only have so much room to move within my present circumstances. And whether I'm ready for it or not, there's more calling me into focus, into evolution, and into creation. Hallelujah!

I don't know where I'm going yet, but I know what I'm choosing. For myself, and for my dogs. I need to provide us with something more structural and grow into the next phase of my journey of life. This day, too, was always coming.

And so I lean in. I give in. This container isn't going to hold the person I'm growing into. And I am being asked to change... again. I'm choosing to see these challenges as another new beginning. And I'm doing it by seeing what opening is here, amidst the uncertainty.

Where is the bliss? Where is the heart? Where is the energy that carries me through? What support do I need here? Can I ask for it?

Keep pedaling. Keep dancing. Keep surrendering.

I'm not stuck. I'm free.

Where this path leads

"What day is it?" asks Pooh.
"It's today," squeaked Piglet.
"My favourite day," said Pooh.
– A. A. Milne[24]

Now, I am sitting ever more deeply and trustingly in life.

I am seeing the new miles ahead on the horizon, chest full of the massive inhale I just built up in the last decade. And I am harvesting all that I have grown FOR that journey.

I am seeing that I am always fed. Even when I don't like what's happening, I allow myself whatever nourishment is being offered by each of my experiences. Especially the painful and confusing ones.

When I do suffer or struggle, I trust myself to lean into it and really listen to what it teaches me about what I need, who I am, who I want to be, the world, and life at large. If only to remind me to breathe.

I breathe more deeply.

I connect with everyone I meet because I've gone deep within myself to find acceptance and compassion.

In the process of loving my circumstances and the events in my life that tore the pretences away, I discovered that I am in everything and everyone. I am more than just "me." So I'm sharing and throwing my own line out to sea, now. Helping and encouraging others teaches me and encourages me, too.

Claiming my truth and my voice as a woman is still hard at times, but I'm finding *my* ways of doing that. I'm surrounding myself with more and more people that give me room to be in the world with what I have to say, with all my intelligence and wisdom, with all my pleasure, and with all my gifts and where they come from.

I feel ever more secure. And I ask for support when I need it now. I've grown a gorgeous new network of absolutely terrific and inspiring human beings on a path for real change and truth in the world. My forests are of a towering and sheltering kind.

I've overcome depression and immobility to such a degree that I maybe spend a few hours very occasionally when I need to, to just touch into those places in me and relax deeply.

And that's ultimately become dense "me time" or "decompression."

This year, 2022, I spent my time and energy growing an abundance of organic and tasty food and am nourished on all levels by it, more than I have ever been. Partnering with soil and seeing plants grow and fruit, grounds me into my body and into beauty and extravagance in a way nothings else does.

I can live off of little money, and I find that I am rich.

I've been led to one of the most beautiful and pristine natural paradises on Earth. I am blessed. And this is because I find oasis everywhere I go, and in everything I see. I create it in whatever home environment I find myself in.

It's all a choice. And I trust my ability to choose – more and more every day.

I'm making choices that are aligned with my bliss and vision of bliss for myself. And I'm taking action and tiny huge steps on those choices every day.

I am healing chronic pain slowly and naturally. I am engaged in yoga. I feel so much more in my body than I ever have.

I am redefining what "work" means. And it's working!

I'm having the best sex of my life because I'm choosing it.

Life is an orgasm. I see so clearly the cyclic nature of my body, of evolution and of all life toward what feels truly good and healthy and helps us grow. I am riding the waves, however choppy and horrifyingly huge sometimes. Giving in IS the way. And what a way it is.

I dance to remind myself.

I maintain a really comfortable and peaceful distance from that which truly doesn't serve my greater good anymore.

I have incredible boundaries with my time, health, body, and emotional output. And there's room to get better too.

There's room for more. SO much more. YES!

And yet... the sight of nature, its sounds and beauty and magnitude for wonder can captivate me for hours. And it's enough.

I love and trust myself. And it's enough.

I'm giving into all that I've deeply desired and living it *now*.

What is here – now – is all there is.

Don't give up, give in

Some people feel the rain.
Others just get wet.[25]

Wanting to die is probably the most taxing thought process I have placed on my life. And yet by leaning into that, and in surviving the *will* to die, I think I was freed. That energy did what it needed to bring me back to life.

Death can look like a lot of things. For me, it was the loss of my closest childhood friends, the relationship to my family as I knew it and I had grown up into, and all that I had worked hard to achieve toward a strong, independent, adult life.

I also lost my mind and my default mode of being in the world. I survived one violent attack, and multiple other assaults on my body, and I lost my power, my voice, and my ability to choose and move through society with ease.

I experienced years of being stripped of my innocence, of beauty, and of kindness toward my sexuality (as most growing young women can and do).

I overcame a physically, emotionally, socially, and verbally abusive relationship.

All this totally obliterated my sense of self and connection in the world. And yet, I was still alive, physically. And there was a space now, for being the creator of a new and more authentic life for me.

I had to be willing to carry myself into my own death and rebirth. I had to be willing to fail miserably so that I can redefine what living a good life is. And I had to be willing to stay true to myself, my beingness, and my experiences. This was and remains the path through for me. Whatever the moment, I keep going into it.

And this is the path of really discovering beauty and love, and that the love and beauty is *me*.

Now that I know, I allow there to be a purpose to everything and everyone in my life, however horrible, horrifying, brief, or drawn out it is.

I am always doing what I can, where I can, and this is enough. It is enough to have faith alone sometimes.

When I surrendered to that kind of love and where it led, more love, more richness appeared. And there's really no reason why I need to push away ANY love I feel, my aliveness, or its accompanying blows to my heart.

Love feels so good! Love is so good. Unrequited love was a gift; the gift of turning that love toward my own heart, and the gift of knowing my heart. And utilizing it to propel me forward.

When I can turn every disappointment into an opportunity to love myself and others more deeply like that, I am free. This is true freedom.

When I am able to let myself go into acceptance, gratitude, and the grace that each of my experiences offers me, I am led into my true self and life. And I know that by how deeply satisfying it feels on all levels, and the interconnectedness with all life that it leads me to.

Many people who read this will have had their own devastating events and/or circumstances in their lives. And I don't believe you have to have lived through any catastrophe to be *alive* and feel the pulse and wave-like nature of that aliveness and how it asks us to grow.

The way I see it:

Simply being birthed into the world is traumatic. It's a wild world.

Our essence is being forced into a mould and into a society and into the wilderness from day 0.

There IS a path to take to come home to our own unique wholeness: this moment.

Often, that path is littered by impacts and challenges, greater or lesser traumatic events and circumstances.

Lean into them. Let them shake you free. Repattern yourself.

Some of the choices we make now will undoubtedly become lessons we will re-work later. **Keep starting a new story. Let that be as glorious as a happy ending.**

Be beaten by the drum of life.

Dance the dance only you know best to the rhythm of those beats.

Freedom comes from loving ourselves through anything and everything.

Love for love's sake allows us detachment from circumstances, but maintain a firm grounding into the present moment, what beauty resides here and is capable of residing here.

What are you living for? Is there something or someone in your life helping you keep going? Teaching you through love?

Follow the gold threads that are shining in the tapestry that surrounds you. Let them lead you.

On the other side, you'll discover you were simply cracking your shell into a birthright of beauty, depth, and abundance.

We all carry the wisdom inside each and every one of us. The journey of life is to go on, learn, live, and love it.

If giving into your suffering with mindfulness for however long it takes – let's say 20 percent of your life – in order to live the rest completely alive, from your own heart, in a state of love, it's worth it.

If it's 50% of your life, it's worth it.

If only for this moment, it's worth it.

You are enough. In fact, you're more than you have the bandwidth to take in sometimes. (wink*) Love what is, and grow that capacity to hold yourself and the abundance of a life lived.

You are beautiful in all your seasons.

Keep going. Don't give up.

This is your one precious life. Give in.

ACKNOWLEDGEMENTS

I am one,
but in that beingness
grows many, many seeds
that have been planted and tended
by the precious heart of Love
that I have found shining
in the many
great ones
that surround me,
with and without your knowledge of it...

Thank you to my gal-pal baby girls, Libby and Mira, for being at my side through it all and giving me a reason to live and to love. You've been some of my biggest support, given me some steep but important mountains to climb, and have always led me to what is better. You and every pet dog on this planet are truly the Earth-bound angels of our time.

Thank you, Chloe. You've been a witness to such a large portion of this story and have been a lamp and a guide through the dark more times than I can count. You've held a sacred space for me. You helped me put sound to my voice and words to my experience that otherwise I would have been too lost to find. You've kept a vision of me as the lotus that I am, and have reminded me of that, again and again. I'm so grateful for you and your support and the capital L – Love – that is YOU in my life.

Thank you, Debbie. Your strength and boldness created the same in me. You were the one that really encouraged to see my story as a gift I can offer others, and fanned my embers into flames when it came to telling it.

Thank you, Rena. Your support I felt as so incredibly authentic and sincere. You are a treasure. Thanks for validating me and carrying me through some of the most important steps of my life.

Thanks, Mel for your steadfast gift of truly helping me, no questions asked, in a moment when I felt like I was grasping at nothing. Thank you for seeing me. Thank you for all the time and energy you've put into being a support for me as I peeled myself off rock bottom one more time and settled back into Truth. Simple, beautiful, animal truth. Thanks babe! ;)

Thank you, Mom. Thanks for all you have provided me over all these years and trusting me to the degree that you could when I severed my old life to start a new one. Thanks for maintaining a deep love for me. Thanks for supporting me to land again, when the time came. Thanks for being yourself, and thus, teaching me to do the same.

Thank you, Dad. Thank you for doing your own personal growth work and showing me my first windows into a yogic and meditative life. Thanks for continually forging our father-daughter bond with your gentle presence and honesty, and being willing to accept my truths, too.

Thank you to my sibs. You are the ones that know me longest and in many ways, closest to my core. You've helped me maintain my connection to innocence, innate worthiness, and that joy from dinner tables keeled over cry-laughing at ourselves. Thanks for loving me each in your own special ways, in all my seasons.

To my family; you've all financially supported me in various ways at some significantly low times over the course of this story. I know it wasn't easy. Thanks for trusting me. Balancing money and healing was at times, a very de-stabilizing part of the process for me, and I'm forever grateful for your gifts.

Thanks, Livs, for always believing in me and what I have to offer the world. Thanks for keeping our connection so strong and sacred while I was going through my dark nights of the soul and wasn't around. Thanks for being there consistently. Thank you and your family for your prayers and your kinship to me. I'm so grateful.

Thank you to all my friends and soulmates. You have come in at all the right times with just the right words to say. If only to show me that I was loved – which is always enough. To all my beautiful and cherished people: Thank you for building new memories with me and reminding me that I, also, am important to your lives. You absolutely know who you are. And if you're wondering if that's you – yes, it's you, too.

Thank you Heather – Etta – for seeing me, inspiring me, and encouraging the gifts in me to flow forth. Your feedback and notes on my manuscript were joys that lit my fire towards its completion. You're so special to me.

Thanks for giving me that first planting job, J. You were the first person to greet me and move me on the other side of my re-birth, and I will always have love and gratitude to you for that.

Thank you, Chantell. You've been such a powerful teacher for me, on and off the dance floor. Wow! You are a force that reaches every corner of this world through the lives that you touch, of this I am sure.

Thank you, Bernice. You have caught me multiple times when I literally had nothing and was living out of my car with my dogs, in order to throw me back onto the dance floor.

Thank you, Alex M. Although I don't mention you in this book, you were my first early signpost toward learning that there is true greatness in virtue, in living from the heart, and in overcoming personal struggles with courage and dignity. So I just want to acknowledge that, here, too.

Thank you, Alexandra Franzen, Lindsey, Woz, and the whole Get It Done gang for giving me this chance, and the community support to complete a project I've wanted to do for several years, now. You all rock! And I am forever fans of yours. Thank you, Tracie, in particular, for giving me such great feedback through the writing process, and gently guiding me into my power to create the manuscript I envisioned for this book.

Thank you, Art, for your eyes and expertise for the final edits of this book. Thanks for your generosity, your praise, and for supporting my work.

Thank you to the trees. Every single one of you. You help me breathe. You help me see the power in slowing down and in growth. You have healed me and you have also made me into a healer. You deserve to stand in a full life, giving and receiving wildly and hugely as you do, each and every one of you. We all deserve that.

Thank you to the first nations and caretakers of this land. This includes since before colonialism and industrialization, and those that are working hard to protect nature and hold sacred our interconnection to all life, today.

Thank you to Love, and the kindness of strangers.

Thank you, Peter.

Thank you to the sisterhood at large.

Thank you, D.

Thank you, J.

Thank you, T.

Thank you to the good men of this world who are loving women well, and making the changes they can in their own lives and the lives around them to make it a safer and better world for everyone.

Thank you to my mentors and teachers.

Thank you to the stars in the sky. You are infinitely and eternally beautiful.

Thank you to the flowers. You are orgasmic-ly inspiring.

Thank you, you, the reader.

Thank you, me.

And on, and on.

Though free to think and act, we are held together, like the stars in the firmament, with ties inseparable. These ties cannot be seen, but we can feel them.
– Nikola Tesla[26]

At some point, giving in becomes giving out.

And I deeply hope that in sharing my story, and in putting it down to start a new one, I give someone else the courage to live from their heart also, to truly know and shape their own story, come what may.

Maybe enough of us can turn this world toward a more beautiful, rich, loving, and surrendered direction. Maybe enough have it in us to deeply and devotedly honour nature, simply by allowing ourselves and what is, to be.

what future hell am I camping in
me right now

Don't Give Up, Give In

REFERENCES & RESOURCES

1 (pg.19) **Carol Barbara Boccaccio**, from a song I wrote titled *Summer Rain* (2018).

2 (pg.27) **F. Scott Fitzgerald** (1896-1940), *This Side of Paradise* (pub. 1920; Charles Scribner's Sons). Originally written as "They slipped briskly into an intimacy from which they never recovered."

3 (pg.30) Author unknown.

4 (pg.33) **Rumi**; Jalāl al-Dīn Muḥammad Rūmī, also known as Jalāl al-Dīn Muḥammad Balkhī (1207-1273) was a 13ᵗʰ century Persian poet, theologian, and Sufi mystic, internationally known for his transcendent poetry and artful teachings.

5 (pg.40) These exercises and courses were featured as part of **Lucy Becker**'s offerings in Toronto, ON. You can find her and her work at www.tantraworkshops.com.

6 (pg.41) **Clarissa Pinkola Estés**, *Women Who Run With The Wolves* (pub. 1992; Ballantine Books); writer, Jungian psychoanalyst, and post-trauma recovery specialist. Also referenced on pg.116.

7 (pg.44) **Lisa Ling** is a writer, journalist, executive producer and host, CNN's *This is Life* and OWN's *Our America*. This quote is from an in-person interview featured in the documentary, *Miss Representation*.

8 (pg.44) **Alice Walker** is a writer and social activist notably known for her novel *The Color Purple* (pub. 1982; Harcourt Brace Jovanovich) which was adapted to the screen in 1985 by Steven Spielberg.

9 (pg.45) **Jean Kilbourne** is a writer, activist, filmmaker, and senior scholar. She created the docuseries *Killing Us Softly*. This quote is from an in-person interview featured in the aforementioned documentary, *Miss Representation*.

10 (pg.46) **American Psychological Association** (2007) www.apa.org/news/press/releases/2007/02/sexualization

11 (pg.46) **Jackson Katz** is an educator, writer and filmmaker. His work includes a documentary called *Tough Guise*, and a book called *The Macho Paradox*. This quote is from an in-person interview featured in the aforementioned documentary, *Miss Representation*.

12 (pg.55), **15**(pg.64), **16** (pg.66), **17** (pg.71) **Steven Hoskinson** is a researcher, post-trauma growth specialist, and the founder of Organic Intelligence®. "He has trained thousands of trauma therapists, health professionals, mindfulness experts, and teachers." – taken from www.organicintelligence.org/steven-hoskinson/. The *End Of Trauma*™ is a course offered through Organic Intelligence®. Also referenced on pg.116.

13 (pg.56) **Osho** (1931-1990); excerpts from talks (*The Divine Melody*) given by Osho. Also knows as Rajneesh, or Bhagwan Shree Rajneesh; an Indian mystic, a teacher in Zen and enlightenment, and a speaker who had a big following in the West. Osho wrote the book *No Water, No Moon* which contains talks on Zen stories and parables about the path to enlightenment. Much of his work and his talks have now been published; this has been made possible thanks to the **Osho International Foundation.** Also referenced on pg.116.

14 (pg.63) **Gabor Maté** is an author, speaker, and physician. He specializes in addiction, trauma, stress and childhood development. This quote is from an article written by Gabor Maté off of his website www.drgabormate.com titled "How to Build a Better Culture of Good Health" (pub. 2015). It first appeared in *yes!* magazine.

15-17 *(see notes for 12,15,16,17)* **Steven Hoskinson.**

18 (pg.73) **Vernon Howard** (1918-1992); quoted from *The Mystic Path to Cosmic Power* (pub. 1967; Parker Pub. Co.) Here, he is paraphrasing teachings from the Taoist philosophers and writers Lao Tzu and Chuang Tzu. Taoism is a school of philosophical thought concerned with the nature of the Universe.

19 (pg.76) **Richard Le Gallienne** (1866-1947) was an English author and poet. The quote is from a poem titled *I Meant To Do My Work To-Day*.

20 (pg.81) **Zora Neale Hurston** (1891-1960) *Dust Tracks On The Road*, autobiography (pub. 1942; J. B. Lippincott). Hurston was an author, anthropologist, and filmmaker. I first heard this from **Maya Angelou** (1928-2014), who was known to quote this saying a lot. Maya Angelou was a memoirist, writer, and civil rights activist. Angelou wrote seven autobiographies including her first publication *I Know Why The Caged Bird Sings*.

21 (pg.85) This is a short poem called *Risk* by **Anais Nin** (1903-1977); a diarist, essayist, novelist, and writer of short stories and erotica.

22 (pg.89) **Bernice Raabis** is a DJ, conscious dance facilitator, mentor, teacher, and expressive arts therapist. She founded *Dance The Medicine*, a coaching platform whose mission is to create more conscious dance spaces internationally.

23 (pg.91) Originally quoted in a book of sayings titled *Salt In My Attic* by **John A. Shedd** (1859-1931); American author and professor. I first came across this quote through Clarissa Pinkola Estés' talks.

24 (pg.93) Excerpt from *Winnie The Pooh* (pub. 1926) by children's book author and poet, **Alan Alexander Milne** (1882-1956).

25 (pg.97) This quote first may have first been coined by **Roger Miller** in 1973. Later it was attributed to musicians, Bob Dylan, and/or Bob Marley.

25 (pg.108) From "The Problem of Increasing Human Energy" first published in 1900 by **Nikola Tesla** (1856-1943); inventor, engineer, and creative mind.

FURTHER RESOURCES

I feel it very valuable and important to share two more resources, my author mentors, and a personal tip for those that may be struggling with past traumatic events and/or PTSD.

Firstly, one can find on YouTube:
"Neurobiology of Trauma and Sexual Assault – Jim Hopper, Ph.D. – July 2015"
This is a free 2-hour presentation provided by a neurobiologist and researcher Jim Hopper on how strong traumatic events affects the brain both during the event, and after. I have found this talk has provided me huge relief, and answers to questions about my own traumatic experiences. This is also a good resource if you work in law enforcement, victim services, or if you plan on reporting a traumatic offence to the authorities.

And, finally, there is another amazing resource I came across just prior to writing this book. I credit it to having really helped validate what I have found to be most helpful on my path of trauma healing. It has given me the chance to open up the bandwidth to pursue my pleasures more seriously, including completing writing this memoir. I've quoted him several times in this book. His name is **Steven Hoskinson**. His research, his offerings, and his work is under the name "Organic Intelligence®" and can be found at the url: **organicintelligence.org**. His approach is unique in the field of trauma in that it takes the focus away from "the problem" (or what is overwhelming) and toward that which the biology finds naturally safe and easeful.

A few authors whose ideas have provided significant mentorship, peace, and relief for my journey include: **Clarissa Pinkola Estés**, **Maya Angelou**, **John O'Donohue**, **Charles Eisenstein**, and **Osho** (Bhagwan Shree Rajneesh).

To all: find consistent, compassionate support in your life. I have been blessed with truly amazing counsellors and important, deep connections with others because I chose to seek them out for my own well-being. You can, too. Be well, friends.

Carol Barbara Boccaccio has been a lover of words ever since she was able to read the lyrics of her father's Beatles and Beach Boys albums. She started journalling when she was a teenager, and has continuously leaned on creative outlets like drawing, singing, dancing, and writing as her deeper mode of life expression. Carol's motivation to grow and heal herself was founded on what was originally a greater desire to heal others. The writing of this memoir has been that; a new port on the sea of self-healing and thus, collective healing. Her greatest accomplishment in life has been braving the unknown, and what it means to embrace consciousness. Carol believes in following her joy and embodying a heartful existence. And that we more aptly shape ourselves and the world by how we are than what we do. Visit her at carolbarbaraboccaccio.com.